JOHN MUIR

At Home in the Wild

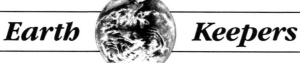

Earth Keepers

JOHN MUIR

At Home in the Wild

Katherine S. Talmadge
Illustrated by Antonio Castro

Twenty-First Century Books

A Division of Henry Holt and Company
New York

Twenty-First Century Books
A Division of Henry Holt and Company, Inc.
115 West 18th Street
New York, NY 10011

Henry Holt® and colophon are registered trademarks of
Henry Holt and Company, Inc.
Publishers since 1866.

Library of Congress Cataloging-in-Publication Data

Talmadge, Katherine S.
John Muir : at home in the wild / Katherine S. Talmadge
Illustrated by Antonio Castro. — 1st ed.
p. cm. — (Earth keepers)
Includes index.
Summary: A biography of the naturalist who founded the Sierra Club and
was influential in establishing the national park system.
1. Muir, John, 1838-1914—Juvenile literature. 2. Naturalists—United
States—Biography—Juvenile literature. 3. Conservationists—United States—
Biography—Juvenile literature.
[1. Muir, John, 1838-1914. 2. Naturalists. 3. Conservationists.]
I. Castro, Antonio, 1941- ill. II. Title. III. Series.
QH31.M9T35 1993
333.7′2′092—dc20 [B] 92-36292 CIP AC

ISBN 0-8050-2123-x
First Edition—1993

Printed in Mexico
All first editions are printed on acid-free paper ∞.

10 9 8 7 6 5 4 3 2 1

Contents

*"Climb the mountains and
get their good tidings."*

Chapter 1

Man of the Wilderness

The icy Alaskan winds were blowing hard when the
tall, thin man with scraggly beard crept away from camp
in early morning. He told the small black dog that followed him to "go back to camp and stay warm. This storm
will kill you." But the dog kept coming.

It was August 1880. The man was John Muir,
America's leading conservationist. His efforts to preserve
the wilderness were well known. So were his theories
about glaciers and the way in which they had helped to
carve out the land. A glacier is a slowly moving mountain
of ice.

John Muir was determined to explore the huge glacier
near the camp. So began one of his most famous adventures, and the tiny dog called Stickeen was a part of that
adventure.

The glacier was about 1,000 feet tall. With an ax, Muir cut a little step in the ice. Once on that step, he cut another one just above. Then he used the steps to climb all the way to the top. Stickeen scrambled up just behind him.

Muir found the glacier was so wide that he couldn't see the other edge. It looked like an endless, shiny white field. It took three hours to cross the top, and they had to jump across deep cracks up to six feet wide. They climbed a second, taller glacier. In late afternoon, they began the long trip back down to camp.

The route coming down was more dangerous than it had been going up. The glacier seemed to be shifting. Muir came to a crack that was 50 feet across. The winds had formed a thin, lacy wire of ice that crossed the crack like a rope bridge. Each end of the bridge began about eight feet down inside the crack. The bridge drooped in the middle, like a hammock.

One thousand feet below, Muir could just make out the floor of the glacier. This string of ice was his only chance to get down off the glacier before nightfall. To stay up there meant freezing to death.

He chopped steps in the steep wall so he could climb down to the bridge. "Life and death were in every stroke" of the ax, he said. Muir chopped away at the sharp, pointed top edge of the bridge to make a flat surface. It was only six inches wide. He gripped the sides of the blue sliver with his knees and hitched forward one or two inches at a time. Then he stretched his arms ahead as far as he could and chipped out a flat surface for his next move. He said, "To me, the edge of that blue sliver was then all the world."

As Muir inched his way across, Stickeen howled and moaned. The dog would not follow him. When he was safely across, Muir called to Stickeen: "Come on, now. You can do it. I know you can."

Stickeen crouched and slid down the cliff on his belly. Then he slowly lifted each of his paws onto the icy thread. Bracing himself against the howling wind, Stickeen crossed, one tiny step at a time. Finally, he joyfully jumped into Muir's outstretched arms.

Although Stickeen belonged to Muir's traveling companion, the dog followed Muir all during that wilderness trip. Years later, John Muir would say it was one of his finest adventures. The huge glacier that he and Stickeen explored together now bears the name Muir Glacier.

John Muir had always been fascinated by nature. The smallest, most fragile wildflower delighted him. Over the years, he wandered through the mountains, down the paths of rivers, and into the icy glacial regions of Alaska. Usually, he carried only a small backpack for collecting plant specimens, a notebook for jotting down thoughts, and a few pieces of dried bread for food.

Years before his adventure with Stickeen, he had come to California to see the jagged, snowcapped Sierra Nevada mountains of Yosemite Valley. On one journey in 1868, John Muir set out on foot to cross the Santa Clara Valley on a 100-mile hike to the Sierras. "It was the bloom-time of the year over the lowlands and coast ranges," he later wrote. "The landscapes of the Santa Clara Valley were fairly drenched with sunshine...and the hills were so covered with flowers that they seemed to be painted."

For days he hiked on. Then he wrote, "At my feet lay the Great Central Valley of California, level and flowery, like a lake of pure sunshine, forty or fifty miles wide."

On the other side of this magnificent natural garden loomed the mighty Sierra mountain range. He described the radiant colors: "Along the top and extending a good way down was a rich pearl-gray belt of snow; below it a belt of blue and dark purple...and stretching along the base of the range a broad belt of rose-purple. All these colors, from the blue sky to the yellow valley smoothly blending as they do in a rainbow, making a wall of light."

John Muir was a learned man and a tireless adventurer. But most important, Muir was a staunch conservationist. Even 100 years ago, he saw that the wilderness might be doomed. He saw fields of wildflowers destroyed when sheep ranchers began to herd their flocks up into the high pastures. He saw lumber companies tearing down the massive forests. He saw cities trying to claim mighty rivers as sources of drinking water.

Muir fought to preserve the wilderness with words. His notebooks were the source of articles and books that described the majesty of nature and the importance of saving it. "Climb the mountains and get their good tidings," he once wrote. "Nature's peace will flow into you as sunshine flows into trees. The winds will blow their own freshness into you, and the storms their energy, while cares will drop off like autumn leaves."

In 1892, John Muir helped to found the Sierra Club and served as its first president. It was established primarily to protect the Sierra mountains that he loved so much. Over the last century, it has become an international organization.

The purpose of the Sierra Club is "to explore, enjoy, and protect the wild places of the Earth; to practice and promote the responsible use of the Earth's ecosystems and resources; to educate and enlist humanity to protect and restore the quality of the natural and human environment; and to use all lawful means to carry out these objectives."

A major belief of the Sierra Club is that the elements of nature—including people—are all connected. "When we try to pick out anything by itself," John Muir wrote many years ago, "we find it hitched to everything else in the universe." Since people are capable of being the greatest source of destruction, Muir believed we have a special responsibility to protect the other elements.

Muir's writings have left us with a vivid picture of what the wilderness regions of the United States looked like almost 100 years ago. Thanks to his tireless conservation work, many of those regions have kept their wildness and are enjoyed by us today.

*"These were . . . the beginnings
of lifelong wanderings."*

Chapter 2

Growing Up

John Muir was born in Dunbar, Scotland, on April 21, 1838. He was the third child born to Daniel and Ann Muir, and was their first son. Later, there would be eight Muir children in all.

The name *Muir* was a good one for young John. In Scottish dialect, it means "moor," a rolling wilderness meadow, home to wildflowers and birds. The grassy moors that stretched over the Scottish landscape were also home to John Muir. He went to the moors whenever he could to watch the birds and to play. His early love for wild, untamed nature would follow him for his whole life.

John started school when he was three years old. But even before that, his grandfather had taught him to read by naming the letters on shop signs.

Young John had bright red hair and sparkling blue eyes. He was an active child who loved to take his younger brother David to explore the meadows and fields. John also loved to climb, and he often practiced climbing at the ruins of 1,000-year-old Dunbar Castle.

"I was so proud of my skill as a climber," he later wrote, "that when I first heard of hell, I always insisted that I could climb out of it. I imagined it was only a sooty pit with stone walls like those of the castle, and I felt sure there must be chinks and cracks in the masonry for fingers and toes."

John's father, Daniel Muir, was a shopkeeper. He was also a very religious man. When he was not working in his store, he read the Bible and warned his children about their adventurous, "evil" ways. He often whipped his children if he found that they were out playing rather than doing their schoolwork and their chores.

As the oldest boy in the family, John was expected to be quiet and responsible. He tried, but the call of the meadows and the thrill of climbing at Dunbar Castle often got him into trouble with his father. His "trips of discovery" into the meadows and hills became a kind of escape from the harsh treatment he received at home. He said of that time in his life:

How our young wondering eyes reveled in the sunny, breezy glory of the hills and the sky....Kings may be blessed; we were glorious, we were free—school cares and scoldings, heart thrashings and flesh thrashings alike, were forgotten in the fullness of Nature's glad wildness. These were my first excursions—the beginnings of lifelong wanderings.

One night when John was ten years old, he and David were doing their homework at their grandfather's house. Suddenly, their father burst into the house and told them he had sold his shop and packed up their belongings. He was taking John, David, and their sister Sarah to America the next day. John's mother and the other four children would join them once Daniel had bought and cleared the land for their farm and built a house.

They boarded a ship on February 19, 1849. Six weeks later, they landed in New York City. Then they went up the Hudson River to Albany and across New York State on the Erie Canal. In Buffalo, they took a steamship across the Great Lakes to Milwaukee, Wisconsin.

Daniel hired a farmer to take them by wagon to the town of Kingston, where he bought 80 acres of deep woods. In one day, Daniel built a small shanty, or hut, to live in while they chopped down part of the woods to make farm fields.

Many years later, John Muir wrote about the day he rode out in an oxcart to his new American home. "Just as we arrived at the shanty," he wrote, "before we had time to look at it or the scenery about it, David and I jumped down in a hurry off the load of household goods, for we had discovered a blue jay's nest. In a minute or so we were up in the tree beside it, feasting our eyes on the beautiful green eggs and beautiful birds—our first memorable discovery."

Clearing part of that wilderness to make a farm was very hard work. With an ox-drawn plow, Daniel ripped up bushes and small trees and then dug up the roots and stumps. John and David piled everything up and burned it. With the help of some local carpenters, they built a farmhouse. It was finished by October, and in November, John's mother and the rest of the family arrived from Scotland.

John was expected to do a heavy load of the farm work. That first winter, he got up every morning at six o'clock. Before breakfast, he fed the horses and cattle, sharpened axes and other tools, chopped firewood, and fetched buckets of water from a nearby stream.

After breakfast, he cut and split logs to make the rails for the fences that would surround each field and pasture. "I used to cut and split a hundred a day," he later wrote, "swinging the axe and heavy mallet, often with sore hands, from early morning to night."

In the spring of 1850, John's father turned another farm chore over to him—guiding the ox-drawn plow. At 12 years of age, John was hardly able to see over the top of the plow handles. Once the plowing was done, John had to plant wheat. In the summer, he had to harvest the wheat. He cut it down and raked it into piles. Then he loaded it onto big wagons, hauled it to the barn, and lifted it into the barn loft. Even when he was seriously ill with the mumps, his father sent him out to work in the fields.

All of the children worked. In the summer, often they "were called in the morning at four o'clock and seldom got to bed before nine, making a broiling, seething day seventeen hours long loaded with heavy work," John wrote.

As they worked, their father most often stayed in the house, reading his Bible. They knew that he would whip them if they dared to take a break from their chores. So there was "no rest in the shade of the trees on the side of the fields," John said.

Because he was forced to spend all his time working, John Muir did not go to school. Somehow, though, he managed to save some money, and when he was 15, he bought an arithmetic book. Every day after lunch, he would steal a few minutes from his chores to study arithmetic. He bought more books and taught himself algebra, geometry, and trigonometry. He also borrowed novels and books of poetry from a neighbor.

At night, John sat in the kitchen and read by candlelight after everyone was asleep. But his father often caught him and ordered him to bed. Finally, John talked his father into letting him get up earlier than the normal winter rising time of six o'clock. He would go to bed at eight o'clock as he was supposed to. But he would get up at one o'clock in the morning and read until six. "Five hours to myself!" he would say with joy. "Five huge, solid hours!"

Soon he began to do other things during this wonderful time of peace and quiet. He would sneak down to the cellar and work with his father's tools.

The first thing he built was a small model of a sawmill. He had never seen one, but he found that he could use the power of the running water in a nearby stream to run a saw and cut boards. And, although he had never seen the inside of a clock, he figured out how to make one. Then he invented machines that used clocks. For example, he invented a timer that would automatically feed the horses by dumping oats and barley into their feed buckets at the right time.

Perhaps his most creative invention was his alarm clock, which he called his "rising machine." The machine had a timer. When the timer went off, a bed would tilt so that a sleeping person would be dumped onto the floor.

His reading and his inventions gave new spirit to John Muir. By the summer of 1860, he was 22 years old. He didn't know what he wanted to do with his life, but he was sure of one thing. He knew he didn't want to be a farmer and live under his father's rules.

The neighbor who had been loaning John his books had an idea. The Wisconsin State Agricultural Fair was coming up in September. At the fair, farmers and tradesmen

would be exhibiting their crops and wares. Why not, the neighbor said to John Muir, make an exhibit of his strange inventions? Surely they would gain him some fame. And they might even land him a job in a factory, far away from wheat fields and strict rules.

So in 1860, John Muir packed up his inventions and his clothes and went off to Madison, the capital of Wisconsin. Before he left, he asked his father to loan him some money for his travel expenses. His father refused, saying, "Depend entirely on yourself."

Chapter 3

Out in the World

John Muir arrived at the Wisconsin State Agricultural Fair with bags and boxes full of his inventions. "Young man, what have we got here?" asked the man in charge of exhibits when he saw John's clocks and thermometer. "Did you make these? They look wonderfully beautiful and novel, and must, I think, prove the most interesting feature of the fair." And so they did. John later wrote that he got "lots of praise from the crowd and the newspaper reporters."

A man named Wiard saw John's exhibit and offered him a job in his iron foundry and machine shop. John accepted the job, but after a few months he felt "desperately hungry and thirsty for knowledge." He wanted to go to the University of Wisconsin. And, even though he had not been to school in 12 years, he so impressed the dean of the university that he was admitted.

He took the courses that most interested him, including chemistry, geology, and botany. Another student at Wisconsin, Milton Griswold, gave John his first formal lesson in botany. One day, Griswold plucked a flower from a nearby locust tree. He challenged John to study the flower and name the family of plants that the locust tree belonged to.

Although John had carefully looked at thousands of wildflowers, he had never considered the connections between one plant and another. But he studied the locust flower and said, "It's like a pea flower."

"You're right," said Griswold. "It belongs to the Pea family." Griswold continued to teach him how plants are classified according to their similar characteristics. After that lesson, John "wandered away at every opportunity" to gather specimens and study them.

John paid his expenses at the university by working at nearby farms and by teaching school in a town ten miles away. He also sold more "rising machines," and to save himself time, he invented a special study desk.

John lined up all his books on a shelf at the back of the desk. Then he rigged up a timer. When he sat down to study, the timer made the first book drop onto the desk, open at the right place. John would read that book for exactly 15 minutes. When the time was up, an arm on the desk would push the book out of the way. The next book would then fall onto the desk for another 15 minutes of study time.

In the summers, he continued to work on nearby farms. On his lunch breaks, he collected wildflowers. Over time, he analyzed and classified all the flowering plants that grew in that region of the country.

While at the university, John Muir formed a lasting friendship with his adviser, Dr. Ezra Slocum Carr, and his wife, Jeanne. Throughout most of his life, Muir would correspond with Mrs. Carr. She proved to be a great help with his career.

After four years at the university, John felt it was time to move on, even though he hadn't taken all the courses he needed to graduate. It was June 1863, and the Civil

War was raging. Young men in the North were being drafted into the Union army. John knew he could not bring himself to fight, so he decided to become a doctor and serve his country by treating the wounded.

John left the university that June. He planned to spend the summer hiking and then start medical school in September. Later, he wrote about his decision to leave the university. "I was far from satisfied with what I had learned, and should have stayed longer. Anyhow, I wandered away on a glorious botanical and geological excursion, which has lasted nearly fifty years and is not yet completed." He also said that he was "only leaving one University for another, the Wisconsin University for the University of the Wilderness."

With two friends, he hiked south, down the banks of the Wisconsin River to the Mississippi. By August, he had returned to Wisconsin with a pack filled with plants, fossils, and a notebook of jottings about the places he had seen.

John expected to work at his sister Sarah's farm until it was time to start medical school at the University of Michigan. But as the date to leave approached, John had spells of "vague unrest and longings." Part of him felt he should become a doctor so that he could help people.

Another part of him wanted only one thing—freedom. He was 25 years old, and the finest moments of his life had been spent alone, in the wilderness.

Finally, John Muir decided to pursue medical school "some other time." All he really wanted to do was continue his "rambles." In the spring of 1864, he left for Canada and began a lifetime journey dedicated to learning about and saving his beloved wilderness.

He explored the country around Lake Huron and Georgian Bay. To earn money, John worked for a time in a factory that made brooms and rakes. While there, he devised machines that doubled the daily output of broom handles. But he was anxious to continue his travels. John wrote to Jeanne Carr that "a lifetime is so little a time that we die ere we get ready to live."

Indianapolis, Indiana, was his next stop. He landed a job with Osgood, Smith & Co., at that time one of the largest producers of carriage parts. He gradually redesigned most of the factory's machines to make them work better and faster.

When a coworker asked John how long he might stay at the factory, he answered, "Just long enough to make a few hundred dollars. Then I am going on with my studies in the woods." However, he delayed leaving and continued to work at the factory into the spring of 1867.

Then a terrible accident changed his life. While using a large metal file to fix a machine, he slipped. The file pierced his right eye. For weeks, John was blind due to the wound in one eye and swelling in the other. He was afraid he would never again see what he loved the most— the meadows, the mountains, and the birds.

Gradually, his sight returned. John realized he had to resume his wanderings and see the things that were important to him, so he left Indianapolis. After staying for a while with his family in Wisconsin, he took a train to Louisville, Kentucky. From there John began a 1,000-mile walk to Florida. "I wandered, afoot and alone," he recalled later, "with a plant-press on my back."

He took few things with him, but one of the most important was a blank notebook. He would fill it with his observations along the way. The many notebooks he filled as he wandered from place to place over the years became the source for the articles and books that later made him famous.

It took John six weeks to reach Florida. After spending some time there, he took a ship to Cuba, where he studied palms and other tropical plants. He planned to go to South

America to explore the Amazon River but became ill with malaria. Malaria is a serious disease carried by mosquitoes. He had caught the disease in the swamps of southern Florida. Too weak to go into the hot climate of South America, John hopped a ship for New York City instead.

The big eastern city depressed him. He thought the busy streets, lined with buildings, looked like "terrible canyons." But he was there for a purpose—New York was the hub of ship travel, and every week ships sailed, bound for exciting new places to explore. People had told him about California and the rugged wilderness of its Yosemite Valley. California had set aside Yosemite as a state park in 1864, and John decided that it would be his next destination.

John Muir boarded a ship for San Francisco and arrived there on March 28, 1868. He asked a stranger for directions to "any place that is wild."

He found that wild place in the Sierra mountains.

"Avalanches were rushing wildly down the narrow side canyons."

Chapter 4

Finding the Range of Light

The sunlight and shadows playing across the Sierras' steep rocky cliffs, sparkling here and there with the spray of thundering waterfalls, thrilled John Muir. The ever-changing colors—bright yellows, dark greens, stark grays, and velvety deep reds and purples—led Muir to name the mountain range "the Range of Light." From the first moment that he saw the mountains in 1868, he was happiest whenever he returned to the Sierras.

That first journey into the California wilderness was a botanist's dream-come-true. John found many plants and trees that he had never seen before. He was awed by the giant sequoia tree, a huge evergreen that grows to a height of about 200 feet.

After that first trip, Muir worked during the fall and winter harvesting crops, tending horses, and herding sheep. He longed to return to the mountains, though, and became lucky—a sheep rancher hired him to accompany a shepherd into the high Sierras with a herd of 2,000 sheep.

Sheep ranchers would drive their herds up into the cool mountains during the spring, when the green grazing meadows of the flat California valleys became parched and dry. So, on June 3, 1869, John began another trek into the high country of the Sierras. His job was merely to lend a hand to the shepherd when needed. For much of the time, he would be free, and yet paid, to wander through the mountains.

John thought sheep were silly, dumb beasts. His dislike for them grew when he saw the herd trample over the fragile mountain valleys, crushing whatever wildflowers they did not gobble down to the roots. He hated to see destruction of the wilderness.

After five days of wandering and grazing, the herd reached the high country. "How deep our sleep last night in the mountain's heart, beneath the trees and stars, hushed by solemn-sounding waterfalls and many small soothing voices in sweet accord whispering peace!" Muir wrote about his first camping experience at the top of the Sierras.

John met a Native American in the wilderness and was struck by how silently the man moved through the forests, making few marks and disturbing no wildlife. It seemed in stark contrast to the destruction the sheep ranchers were causing by using the wilderness as grazing land. "Indians walk softly and hurt the landscape hardly more than the birds and squirrels," he wrote with respect.

The six-week shepherding job ended all too quickly for Muir. In the fall, having earned more "biscuit and tea" money, he returned to the Sierras, determined to stay through the icy winter months. He made friends with J. M. Hutchings, who had a hotel in the upper Yosemite valley.

John built himself a cabin, and he let a stream run right through it. That way, ferns, frogs, and rippling water were always his companions. Then he and Hutchings set up a water-powered sawmill to cut trees that had fallen in the fierce autumn windstorms.

John stayed at the cabin and worked at the sawmill for two full years. But he still found time to study and catalog the plants, animals, and insects. He even discovered a new species of butterfly, which was eventually named after him.

Muir became very interested in the unstable weather patterns of the Sierras and Yosemite Valley. He was particularly interested in the drama of storms. "I was awakened in the morning by the rocking of my cabin and the beating of pine-burs on the roof," he wrote about one particularly heavy snowstorm. "Avalanches were rushing wildly down the narrow side canyons...with loud resounding roar...making the whole valley vibrate as though it were an instrument being played."

His interest in icy storms naturally led John Muir to study glaciers.

Glaciers are huge rivers of ice, often several miles wide and thousands of feet deep. On the top, they look like icy mountains. But deep inside, they are more liquid. They ooze and move very slowly over the land, at a rate of about a mile a year. On their way, they grind rocks, uproot trees, and carve out the land.

A million years ago, glaciers covered much of the world. Their movement carved out the valleys, rivers, lakes, and oceans that we know today. Gradually, the heat of the earth melted the glaciers, and they disappeared. There are only a few small glaciers still in existence, in the coldest regions of the earth.

Muir found over 60 small glaciers, about 30 feet deep, high up in the Sierras. He believed that the mountains had been formed when glaciers came through long ago, grinding out steep valleys in their path.

Based on his studies of the Yosemite glaciers, Muir wrote an article entitled "The Death of a Glacier" and sent it off to the New York *Tribune*. It was published in December 1871. The magazine's readers were enthusiastic, and the magazine asked for more articles.

Over the next five months, John wrote more articles, titled "Yosemite in Winter" and "Yosemite in Spring." He was gaining the respect of scientists for his geological studies. At the same time, he was gaining a large audience of readers who turned to his articles to learn about the natural beauty of the Sierra wilderness.

Muir could already see that the wilderness was facing a threat. Through the efforts of the California State Park Commission, Yosemite Valley had been "discovered" by campers and tourists. Now hotels, campgrounds, and trails had begun to appear. In the process of development, a good deal of land was cleared of trees. As a result, there was a terrible flood in Yosemite Valley that winter.

Again, John wrote an article, called "Yosemite Valley in Flood." In it, he severely criticized the California State Park Commission for destroying the natural beauty of Yosemite in the course of "improving" it. It was his first public outcry as a conservationist.

Muir's need to study glaciers in the "undiscovered" wilderness led him to nearby Hetch Hetchy Valley. Though smaller than Yosemite Valley, it contained magnificent sheer cliffs rising above a fertile green valley. He said Hetch Hetchy was "one of Nature's rarest and most precious mountain temples."

In Hetch Hetchy, as in Yosemite Valley, he found more evidence to support his glacial theories concerning the formation of cliffs and valleys. He wrote, "Yosemite is one of *many*, one chapter of a great mountain book written by the same pen of ice."

Although modern scientists have now proved Muir's glacial theories to be true, many scientists in the early 1870s disagreed with him. At that time, the more respected theory was that the valleys were created when great prehistoric earthquakes caused the bottoms of mountains to drop away into the center of the earth. This theory

was so well accepted that when a huge earthquake hit Yosemite on March 26, 1872, most people fled the area, fearing that the bottoms of the mountains would drop out even further.

Muir saw the theory as nonsense. He believed that earthquakes caused rock slides, which changed only the ragged surfaces of the mountains. So he, unlike the others, did not run away as the earthquake began. Instead, in characteristic style, he stayed to watch.

It was two o'clock in the morning. He ran out of his cabin, feeling sure he was "going to learn something." The land was moving and shaking so violently that Muir had to balance as if walking on the deck of a ship tossing on the sea. It was a moonlit night, and for the first minute or two he heard no sound except a muffled underground rumbling and a slight rustling of the trees.

The silence was brief. "Suddenly," he wrote, "there came a tremendous roar. The Eagle Rock, a short distance up the valley, had given way, and I saw it falling in thousands of the great boulders I had been studying for so long, pouring to the valley floor." The friction of the splitting rocks made a firestorm of sparks "as steady as a rainbow in the midst of the stupendous roaring rock storm."

After the earthquake, Muir found huge forests flattened and destroyed by the rock slides. He found streams that had been dammed up into ponds by falling boulders. But the bottoms had not fallen out of the mountains, as people who opposed his glacial theory had predicted. Instead, the earthquake had dramatically changed the surface features of the land. He published his report and once again spoke of his glacial theory for the formation of mountain valleys.

Muir's glacial studies took him higher and higher into the Sierra mountains. In August 1872, he found a glacier on top of Mount McClure. He planted five stakes in the glacier, and when he returned 46 days later, he found that all the stakes had moved down the mountain. This experiment proved that the ice and snow on the mountain's top were part of a flowing glacier.

Jeanne Carr encouraged John to write about his experiences. Now every glacial experiment and every climbing event became the basis for his articles, which were widely published in several magazines.

More and more, Muir was speaking out against the destruction of the wilderness. In 1873, he took on his old enemy, the sheep, when he wrote, "The grass is eaten close and trodden until it resembles a corral." He went on to say that laws should be passed to keep the sheep out of the Sierra wilderness. He also demanded that attention be paid to the preservation of the giant sequoia trees. Muir was devastated when he saw scars in the trees, left by tourists who were "hacking off chips and engraving their names in all styles."

John Muir's wanderings, begun as a glorious personal escape into nature, were now making him famous. Supporters in nearby San Francisco urged him to "come down from the mountains" and make public appearances and speeches. Occasionally, he did go. But the city depressed him, and he would return to the mountains as soon as he could.

However, on one visit to San Francisco in the spring of 1874, he met John Strentzel, the owner of a large fruit ranch. More important, he met Strentzel's 27-year-old daughter, Louie. John was a confirmed bachelor of 36, but he was attracted to Louie. When invited to visit again, he said he would return.

"Mountain parks and reservations are . . . fountains of life."

Chapter 5

Beyond Yosemite

Muir's growing affection for Louie Strentzel, together with the increasing interest by the public in hearing him speak about conservation, led him to travel out of the mountains more and more frequently.

In January 1875, Muir spoke at the Literary Institute of Sacramento on the destruction of the wilderness environment. The destruction was caused not only by sheep ranchers and tourists but by miners and loggers as well. He felt the California state government was standing by and just letting the wilderness go. He argued for state laws to protect the forests from large-scale timber cutting and from forest fires that were being deliberately set to clear the wilderness for grazing.

That summer, he returned to the Sierras to write a series of articles. In a grove of giant sequoias, he found that one of the largest trees had just been chopped down. The tree had lived for more than 2,000 years, undisturbed. But it had been cut down so that a section of it could be displayed at the 1876 Centennial Exposition in Philadelphia. John was saddened that the tree had been so wasted.

In a grove by the Kings River, John found the charred stump of a giant sequoia. By his estimate, the tree was more than 4,000 years old. Many such trees were being

fed into a busy sawmill close by. If laws were not passed to protect the sequoias, they would surely disappear. "Mountain parks and reservations are useful not only as fountains of timber," Muir wrote in protest, "but as fountains of life."

Although he was very busy, John managed to continue his glacial studies at Yosemite and Hetch Hetchy valleys over the next few years. In 1879, he traveled to Alaska to explore other glaciers and spotted a large one that he was determined to return to. But he put that off for almost a year while he returned to his lecture schedule and to his personal life.

On April 14, 1880, Muir married Louie Strentzel, one week before his forty-second birthday. He then attempted to settle down to a life free of wandering and worked hard to become a successful fruit grower. But as always, farm work was drudgery for him, and life back on the farm made him restless.

His wife, concerned for his health and happiness, came to a generous agreement with him. Every summer, when the crops were ripening, he would be free to take a trip into the wilderness, as long as he returned in time to run the fall harvest. So in late July, Muir left on his first summer excursion—back to Alaska to explore that huge glacier.

He hired a group of Native Americans to guide him along his route to the glacier. He also persuaded his friend S. Hall Young, a missionary, to come along. They loaded their gear into a canoe and were about to start off. At the last moment, Young's small black dog, Stickeen, jumped on board. It was on this trip that Muir and Stickeen crossed the icy glacial bridge.

The expedition gave Muir more data for his glacial research and a welcome break from farm life. But once back in California, he settled into the fruit-growing business again. In March 1881, a daughter, Annie Wanda, was born.

That fall, California Senator John F. Miller asked Muir to act as a consultant for environmental legislation. Miller hoped to put through two new laws. The first was designed to extend the boundaries of Yosemite to protect its forests and lakes. Cities were beginning to look to Yosemite's lakes and waterfalls as possible sources of drinking water and hydroelectric power.

The second law was aimed at creating a new national park in the Yosemite region to protect, among other features, the giant sequoia trees that Muir had written about. Muir threw himself into the effort, but the California state congress eventually turned the bills down.

Muir felt defeated and turned away from further environmental work for almost ten years. He concentrated on his now thriving fruit business and his family. He delighted in taking Wanda through the fields and meadows, teaching her the names of every flower and insect they found.

It was a different relationship, certainly, than he had had with his own father. John had not seen his father in many years. He decided, after writing to his brother David in December 1884, that he would go east for a visit. But duties on the farm prevented a trip until the following summer.

In September 1885, Muir arrived at the home of his sister Joanna in Kansas City. He had already persuaded most of his other brothers and sisters to join him. His stern father, now more than 80 years old, was very ill. John felt great sadness as he sat by his father's bed. Old Daniel Muir raised his head and asked, "Is this my dear John? My dear wanderer." John was by his side when he died on October 6.

A few months later, back in California, Louie gave birth to their second daughter, Helen. The baby was sickly, and Muir stayed at the farm almost continuously for the following two years. He turned to writing again, accepting a publisher's assignment to write a two-volume book entitled *Picturesque California.*

The writing did not come easily, and he became restless and ill. He took a brief trip up the Pacific Coast for relief and decided to climb Mt. Rainier in Washington. Muir wrote to his wife with new vigor and excitement, telling her how thrilling it was to be back climbing amid glaciers in the lofty mountains. She wrote back, saying that a farm that kept a person from doing the important work of his life was not worth keeping. "You need to be your own self, well and strong," she wrote to him.

They decided to hire a manager for the fruit farm. Now John could put all his effort into preserving Yosemite and the Sierras.

"Any fool can destroy trees."

Chapter 6

The Crusade

For several months in 1889, Muir lived in San Francisco, working on the remaining chapters of *Picturesque California.* Then one day, Robert Underwood Johnson, the editor of *Century Magazine*, paid Muir a visit. *Century Magazine* had published a number of Muir's articles. Muir suggested that they take a brief trip to Yosemite Valley.

The valley was a mess. Under the control of the California State Park Commission, the meadows had been plowed to make hay fields for horses. Forests had been destroyed by lumber companies, and sheep ranchers had ruined the hills by overgrazing. Johnson was as saddened as Muir and suggested that the two of them work together to save Yosemite from further destruction.

Muir agreed to write two articles for *Century.* The first would describe the remaining wilderness beauty of

Yosemite. The second would urge readers to rally around the cause, persuading the United States government to make Yosemite a national park.

They knew that it would be difficult to take the control of the existing state park away from California. Instead, they proposed to create a large national park all around the borders of California's state park. National control of at least the outskirts of the region would make it more secure. The laws that created Yellowstone National Park in 1872 also provided for the preservation of its forests, trees, and water resources. Muir and Johnson hoped to persuade Congress to do the same for Yosemite.

Before writing his *Century* articles, Muir drew a map of what he wanted Yosemite National Park to contain. It included the Hetch Hetchy Valley and the groves of giant sequoia trees. He also drew a map of another area further south, where there were many other groves of giant sequoia trees.

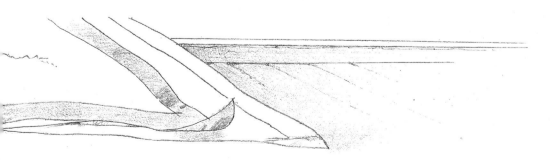

Muir sent his maps to Johnson, who got them to U.S. Representative William Vandever. Shortly thereafter, Vandever presented Congress with a bill to establish Yosemite National Park. But the boundaries that he proposed greatly reduced the area to about one-fifth of what Muir had suggested. Muir wrote to Johnson and argued that the bill would not protect the most valuable, rugged terrain of Yosemite Valley. Johnson then urged Congress to accept Muir's original plan.

Meanwhile, Muir completed his two *Century* articles and went off on a two-month trek across Alaska's Muir Glacier. This was the place where he and the dog Stickeen had crossed the ice bridge nine years earlier.

By the time he returned to California in September 1890, his articles had appeared in *Century* and had created quite a conflict. Supporters of his point of view were sending letters to Congress urging the creation of Yosemite National Park.

However, there were also a number of people against Yosemite National Park, including, of course, the miners, loggers, and farmers. Furthermore, a U.S. Geological Survey engineer had picked Hetch Hetchy Valley as an excellent place to flood in order to build a reservoir. The reservoir would take care of the growing water needs of San Francisco and nearby farming areas, but it would destroy the valley. The Hetch Hetchy conflict would plague Muir for years to come.

In late September, Congress established Sequoia National Park and General Grant National Park, thus putting under federal protection Muir's groves of sequoia trees. Now it was against federal law for lumber companies to chop them down.

Muir's triumph was finally complete on October 1, when Congress established Yosemite National Park. The boundaries were almost exactly the same as those on his original map.

Congress passed another important law in 1891. It gave the president the power, without having to get congressional approval, to protect any parcel of government-held land as a forest reservation. Lumber companies could not cut trees on any such lands. Under the new law, President Benjamin Harrison set aside 13 million acres of forest and named it the Sierra Forest Reserve. Thus, Johnson and Muir had succeeded in protecting a large portion of the Sierras.

Johnson urged Muir to go a step further and to establish an association of private citizens to protect the entire Sierra region from further destruction. It was clear that private interests would continue their efforts to undo Muir's conservation accomplishments. Perhaps, Johnson reasoned, an association would have greater strength and provide national support.

On May 28, 1892, the association was officially created. It was called the Sierra Club. John Muir was its first president and remained so until his death. Today, the Sierra Club has grown to become a protector of worldwide natural resources, rugged expanses of wilderness, and endangered animals.

Muir, at least for the moment, had won. His articles had drummed up popular support for the conservation

of Yosemite, Hetch Hetchy, and the giant sequoias. Committed mountaineers and conservationists were joining the Sierra Club, expanding his base of support. Yet, John was exhausted and, once again, restless.

An old friend, artist William Keith, talked Muir into a trip to Europe in 1893. He visited his old hometown of Dunbar in Scotland and walked through the meadows surrounding the crumbling walls of Dunbar Castle, which he had climbed as a little boy. He traveled on to Norway, finding delight in the glaciers there, and then on to Switzerland's majestic snow-covered Alps.

Back in California that fall, Muir felt refreshed and set to work on a book titled *The Mountains of California*. He had great success with this book and gained widespread support for the Sierra Club. John Muir was now respected as the leading western conservationist and was popularly called "The Father of the National Parks."

In 1896, President Grover Cleveland created the National Forestry Commission. This group of distinguished scientists were to inspect the forest reserves created so far and recommend future goals for protecting America's natural resources. Muir was an adviser to the six commissioners. He traveled with them through the forests of the West and helped write their final report. At the commission's suggestion, in 1897, President Cleveland moved to set aside 13 new forest reserves—21 million acres.

However, President Cleveland left office shortly afterwards. His successor, William McKinley, sided more with the interests of miners, loggers, and other industrialists than he did with environmentalists. Cleveland's decrees were postponed.

Muir was furious. He and members of the Sierra Club began an ambitious campaign of writing magazine articles and letters to government officials. "Any fool can destroy trees" Muir wrote in the *Atlantic Monthly.* "They cannot run away; and if they could, they would still be destroyed—chased and hunted down as long as fun or a dollar could be got out of their bark hides."

The McKinley administration remained insensitive to the need to protect not only forests but also water. Early in 1901, President McKinley signed a bill that would allow California to enter even the nationally controlled region of Yosemite to construct dams and reservoirs.

The national mood switched quickly in September 1901, when Theodore Roosevelt became president. Three months after taking office, Roosevelt proclaimed to Congress, "Forest and water problems are perhaps the most vital internal questions of the United States at the present time." Here, at last, was a president who valued the conservationist point of view of John Muir.

Roosevelt wrote a letter to John Muir, asking Muir to guide him on a hike through the Sierras. "I do not want anyone with me but you, and I want to drop politics absolutely for four days, and just be out in the open with you," the president wrote.

In May 1903, Theodore Roosevelt spent four days alone with Muir in California. They camped out under the stars and the giant sequoias, and Roosevelt listened as Muir talked on and on.

Looking back on the experience, Muir later said, "I stuffed him pretty well, regarding the timber thieves, and the destructive work of the lumbermen, and other spoilers of the forest." He also urged Roosevelt to take the last bit of Yosemite away from the state of California and make the entire region a national park.

Muir's concern for the wilderness inspired Roosevelt to take decisive action. After leaving Muir, Roosevelt made a speech in Sacramento, the state capital of California. He said, "Lying out at night under those giant sequoias was lying in a temple built by no hand of man, a temple grander than any human architect could by any possibility build, and I hope for the preservation of the groves of giant trees simply because it would be a shame to our civilization to let them disappear."

During his administration, Roosevelt set aside 148 million acres of forest reserves. He also set aside 50 regions for the protection of wildlife, created five new national parks, and founded 16 national monuments. Most important to John Muir, Roosevelt was a strong ally in keeping dams out of Hetch Hetchy Valley and in achieving the unification of Yosemite National Park.

The Sierra Club led the battle for the unification. In 1905, John Muir and William Colby, the secretary of the

Sierra Club, presented a bill to the California legislature. The bill outlined plans for the state to give back to the federal government the part of Yosemite that was still a state park. After a long debate, the bill finally passed.

It was a great triumph for John Muir, but the triumph came at a time of great personal tragedy. His wife Louie suddenly became very ill and died on August 6, 1905. Unable to work or to write, Muir went to Arizona to live with his daughters. He stayed there for a long time in a state of grief.

Meanwhile, the California bill went before the United States Congress and met another tough fight. Some representatives feared the high costs of maintaining such a large park. Others were concerned about reserving so much land when it might be needed for water supplies, railroad lines, and other uses. After a long year of argument, debate, and compromise, the bill passed. President Roosevelt signed a new law on June 11, 1906, making all of Yosemite Valley a united national park at last.

But the triumph for the Sierra Club and John Muir was brief because the growing city of San Francisco desperately needed water. And John Muir soon faced his last great battle—to save Hetch Hetchy Valley.

Chapter 7

The Final Battle and Ongoing Legacy

Many people agreed with John Muir that Hetch Hetchy Valley was even more beautiful than Yosemite Valley. No hotels, sheep ranches, or sawmills had ever marred its natural ruggedness. John Muir described a day there this way:

> *It is a sunny day in June, the pines sway dreamily, and you are shoulder-deep in grass and flowers. Looking across the valley through beautiful open groves you see a bare granite wall 1,800 feet high rising abruptly out of the green and yellow vegetation and glowing with sunshine, and in front of it the fall, waving like a downy scarf, silver bright, burning with white sun-fire.*

The Californians saw that waterfall not as a "downy scarf" but as a tremendously powerful source of fresh water. By building a dam at the other end of the valley, they could create a huge lake.

Muir felt that Hetch Hetchy was finally safe, now that the entire Yosemite region was a national park. Then two things happened to threaten Hetch Hetchy. First, there was a terrible earthquake and fire in San Francisco in 1906,

making its need for an abundant water supply more critical. Second, Ethan Allen Hitchcock, Roosevelt's secretary of the interior, resigned. He was replaced by James R. Garfield, who felt that California's water problems were more important than the preservation of wilderness.

Muir, Roosevelt, the Sierra Club, and thousands of American citizens pointed to many other potential sites for a reservoir—places with just as much water but without the beauty of Hetch Hetchy. But Hetch Hetchy appealed to Californians because it was already public land, and therefore the city of San Francisco would not have to buy it.

In 1909, Theodore Roosevelt left office. The new president, William Howard Taft, seemed to be on the side of the conservationists, too. In October, he hiked in Yosemite with Muir. A few days later, Taft's secretary of the interior, Richard Ballinger, went to Hetch Hetchy with Muir. Taft and Ballinger promised they would do everything they could to save the valley.

Confident that the dam would not be built, Muir went back to his writing. During the next three years, he wrote several very successful books, including *Stickeen* and *The Yosemite*. And at the age of 73, he finally got to South America and journeyed down the Amazon River.

He arrived home in California in April 1912. President Taft had kept his promise. All requests from California to build a dam at Hetch Hetchy had been firmly turned down. Then, in 1913, Woodrow Wilson became president. His secretary of the interior was Franklin K. Lane, from San Francisco. Now the city, not the conservationists, had a powerful ally.

Muir and the Sierra Club fought hard to save Hetch Hetchy and received support from all over the country. But in September, the U.S. House of Representatives passed a bill that would let California flood Hetch Hetchy Valley.

Muir kept his hopes up—the bill still had to be approved by the Senate. In November, he wrote to his daughter Helen, "I still think we will win. Anyhow I'll be relieved when it's settled, for it's killing me."

But the Senate did approve the Hetch Hetchy dam. President Wilson signed the bill into law on December 19.

Today, Hetch Hetchy Valley is gone. A large, fenced reservoir stands in its place. Modern scientists and economists agree that it was a terrible mistake.

Muir's friends and associates have said that the loss of that final battle broke John Muir. He spent the next two years writing books, leading the Sierra Club, and visiting his daughters and grandchildren. But his health was failing. He traveled to Arizona to visit his daughter Helen for the Christmas holidays in 1914 but became ill and was sent to a hospital in Los Angeles. He died there on Christmas Eve.

John Muir believed that wilderness areas should stay wild. He fought for this belief most of his life, mainly through his books and articles.

His spirit lives on through his writings. They bring to new generations a sense of the wonder of America's wilderness areas and the challenge to preserve them.

Muir's spirit lives on in the places that bear his name. For example, in the Sierras of California, there are Mt. Muir, Muir Pass, Muir Gorge, and Muir Lake. Outside of San Francisco, a grove of giant redwoods is called Muir Woods National Monument. Two glaciers have been named for him, one on top of Mt. Rainier in Washington and the one in Alaska where he and Stickeen had their adventure.

Muir's spirit lives on in the efforts of the Sierra Club to educate the public about wilderness areas and to preserve them.

Perhaps the "monument" to John Muir that would mean the most to him was created shortly after his death. The Sierra Club persuaded the state of California to construct a rugged mountain trail high in the Sierra mountains so that others could walk in his steps. The trail was completed in 1938.

Today, the John Muir Trail stretches 212 miles, from the top of 14,494-foot Mount Whitney to the heart of Yosemite Valley. Along the way, it crosses a number of other mountains over 14,000 feet in height. Many people have traveled over all or part of this trail to see what John Muir described so vividly in his notebooks.

John Muir's writings inspired the beginnings of conservation. Many years ago, he wrote, "The morning stars still sing together, and the world, not yet half made, becomes more beautiful every day."

Muir believed it is never too late to become involved in conservation. Today, the world is still beautiful, and more than ever, its beauty is in need of protection. Muir would urge us to join in the fight to save for future generations the beauty we have inherited.

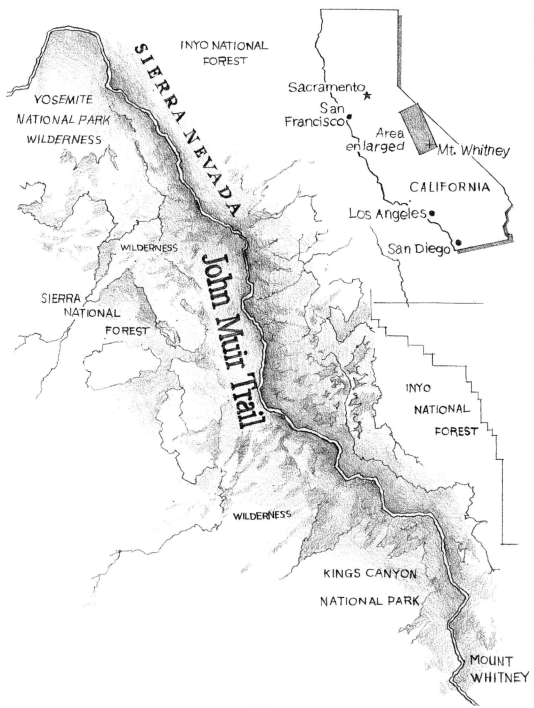

SIERRA NEVADA

INYO NATIONAL FOREST

YOSEMITE
NATIONAL PARK
WILDERNESS

John Muir Trail

WILDERNESS

SIERRA
NATIONAL
FOREST

WILDERNESS

KINGS CANYON

NATIONAL PARK

MOUNT
WHITNEY

Sacramento

San
Francisco

Area
enlarged

Mt. Whitney

CALIFORNIA

Los Angeles

San Diego

INYO

NATIONAL

FOREST

Glossary

agriculture the science of producing crops and raising animals; farming

algebra the mathematical subject in which symbols, usually letters of the alphabet, represent numbers

botany the scientific study of plants

chemistry the science that deals with the composition, structure, and properties of substances and with the changes they undergo

conservation the process by which natural resources are saved

earthquake a shaking or trembling of the earth

ecosystem the network of relationships among living things and their environment

environment the physical world that surrounds a plant or animal

geology the scientific study of the history and structure of the earth

geometry the mathematical subject dealing with the measurement and relationships of lines, shapes, and solid objects

glacier a large formation of ice capable of movement

hydroelectric creation of electricity through the use of energy from running water

locust an animal in the grasshopper family that often damages vegetation and crops

lowlands an area of land lower than the surrounding area

malaria a contagious disease caught from the bite of infected mosquitoes

moor a broad piece of land that is often high and damp

range an extensive area of land; a chain of mountains

reserve, reservation a tract of public land set aside for a special purpose

reservoir a body of water collected and stored for future use

sequoia a very large evergreen tree

species a group of similar plants or animals that can produce offspring

specimen a sample of something taken for study

survey a detailed inspection of an area

trigonometry the mathematical subject dealing with the numerical relationships between the sides and angles of triangles

terrain a geographical area, or the physical features of a tract of land

wilderness an area of land left in its natural condition

wildlife animals or plants living in a natural state

Index